Teen Sunshine
Reflections

Also by June Cotner

Amazing Graces

Animal Blessings

Bedside Prayers

Bless the Day

Family Celebrations

Get Well Wishes

Graces

The Home Design Handbook

Mothers and Daughters

Teen Sunshine Reflections

Words

for

the

Heart

and

Soul

JUNE COTNER
HARPERCOLLINS*PUBLISHERS*

Library of Congress Cataloging-in-Publication Data
Teen sunshine reflections : words for the heart and soul / June
Cotner.
    p.   cm.
    Includes index.
    Summary: An interfaith collection of poems, prayers, and
reflections that address challenges faced by teens, and that includes
words from Mother Teresa, Mahatma Gandhi, the Dalai Lama, and
teenaged authors.
    ISBN 0-06-000525-4 — ISBN 0-06-000527-0 (pbk.)
    1. Conduct of life—Quotations, maxims, etc.—Juvenile
literature. 2. Conduct of life—Literary collections—Juvenile
literature. [1. Conduct of life—Quotations, maxims, etc.
2. Quotations. 3. Conduct of life—Literary collections. 4. Youths'
writings.] I. Cotner, June, date.
PN6084.C556 T44 2002   2001051739
082—dc21   CIP
                                                     AC

Typography by Amy Ryan

1 2 3 4 5 6 7 8 9 10

First Edition

In honor and memory of

Spencer Darin Cox
(1984–2001)

You are deeply missed.

A LETTER TO READERS

When I reflect on my teenage years, I still remember how challenging they were. My friends, ideas, body, and lifestyle were all quickly changing, and suddenly it seemed like adults, especially members of my family, were impossible to relate to. I remember feeling restless, and I longed to graduate from high school. I often daydreamed about how wonderful life would be when I turned eighteen and could live on my own — with only myself to answer to.

Looking back now, I wish I had appreciated those years more when I was living them instead of focusing so much on the future. I say this because I have some truly great memories from my teen years. I had my first job (picking peaches); I competed in a number of sports (track, volleyball, and basketball); I had my first date, then eventually my first boyfriend; I got my driver's license (oh, the freedom!); and I made some really great friends, whom I still see when I return to my hometown. I recall attending night football games with my friends. Surrounded by the excitement and energy in the air, we talked and laughed the whole way through and came up with pranks to play on the guys.

It hasn't been too long since I "re-experienced" the teen years through my two children, who are now in their early twenties. I know that today teens are dealing with issues that are very tough, such as drugs, pregnancy, STDs, depression, gangs, and violence. My generation dealt with some of these issues when we were teens, but not at the same level. During these difficult times (or when you simply want inspiration), I hope the selections in this book will provide you with comfort, motivation, encouragement, or just a positive thought that might make your day easier.

In working with more than one hundred teens while compiling this book, I noticed something very remarkable. Your generation is the brightest, most well-informed, and most realistic group I have ever met. You are not afraid to communicate what you think and feel; I find this refreshing. Today teenagers seem to embrace individuality and diversity more than in any other generation. This is so wonderful to see!

I am sure you must get discouraged with how teens are often portrayed in the media as being violent, irrational, and impulsive. My wish for you is that you stay true to your heart and self. I pray you never feel lost or alone along your path to adulthood. And I hope that, in some small way, *Teen Sunshine Reflections* will help you recognize how truly special you are — because our world really needs *you* — your talents, your hopes, your dreams, your ideas, and your positive energy!

THANKS

I owe overwhelming thanks to the teens involved with this book. *Teen Sunshine Reflections* would not have been created without the contributions of talented new teen poets. You would be proud to know that your words survived our review of over three thousand submissions. After I selected my favorite pieces, two teens, Gemma Arcangel and Chelsea Lye, worked very hard to let me know which selections would appeal to their friends. To broaden the feedback for this book, a twenty-member teen panel from across the country read through the "test market" manuscript and gave me their opinions on which poems should be included in the book. Thank you to Emmanuel Arcangel, Gemma Arcangel, Katie Bonacini, Charlie Bowman, Alex Brooks, Kathryn Byron, Eryn Edlund, Caitlin Flannery, Becca Hall, Laura Hall, Ashleigh Howard, Chelsea Lye, Gregory T. Meghani, Lacey Menne, Jared Orr, Megan Smaaladen, Christopher Tolentino, Daniel Wilhelm, Katie Wilhelm, and Laura Younger. I learned a lot from your honest feedback and appreciate your answers to my many questions to make sure our final selections appeal to teens.

I am very thankful to my editor, Barbara Lalicki, for being such a pleasure to work with—I love your tremendous enthusiasm, encouragement, and commitment to excellence. Thanks as well to associate editor Rachel Orr for working so hard on this book and contributing many great ideas, to Leann Reinecke for her feedback, to Josette Kurey for all her help with publicity, and to the rest of the staff at HarperCollins who worked hard to make this book one teens could use.

As always, I feel so blessed to have such a superb literary agent, Denise Marcil. I am forever grateful for all you do!

A tender thank-you goes to my husband, Jim. You fill my life with happiness and devotion. I am eternally grateful for my two children, Kyle and Kirsten—you never fail to make me laugh and always make me feel so loved.

My deepest appreciation goes to my gifted assistants in the office—Cheryl Edmonson (book production and overall office management), Rebecca Pirtle (obtaining permissions and coordinating my publicity events), and Gemma Arcangel (rating teen poems, typing, filing, and running errands). The three of you have contributed immeasurably to the quality of my anthologies. Plus, I love working with each of you!

Recently, another member has joined my staff—my daughter, Kirsten Cotner. She has just graduated from college with a degree in communications. It is such a joy and a dream come true to have you work with me! Your youthful insights helped tremendously in making this book relevant to teens. I look forward to creating many books with you.

Additionally, I would like to express deep gratitude to Father Paul Keenan, Rabbi Rami M. Shapiro, and Reverend Lynn James for giving a careful critique of the manuscript and helping ensure that the book reflected the interfaith quality I desire. I appreciate all of your helpful comments!

My thanks go to all those in the local community who give me such terrific support—the staff at both the Poulsbo and Kingston libraries, who have obtained a number of reference books for me; and Suzanne Droppert, owner of Liberty Bay Books, who provides such strong support for my books.

I'm tremendously grateful to my awe-inspiring "regulars"—poets who have contributed to my books for years now. The following poets also provided their literary expertise and gave thorough critiques—Corrine De Winter, Lori Eberhardy, and Arlene Gay Levine.

A genuine thanks goes out to all the poets who contributed but did not make the final cut. I thoroughly enjoyed reading your submissions and I hope you will continue sending me your work for future books. Never be discouraged!

Finally, I would like to thank God for blessing me with the gift of life—and giving me work I truly love.

OUR TEEN PANEL

Left row:
Emmanuel Arcangel,
Gemma Arcangel,
Katie Bonacini
Middle row:
Charlie Bowman,
Kristen Eryn Edlund,
Becca Hall,
Laura Hall
Right row:
Caitlin Mariah Flannery,
Ashleigh Howard

Left row:
Chelsea Lye,
Gregory T. Meghani,
Lacey Menne
Middle row:
Jared Orr,
Megan Smaaladen,
Christopher Tolentino,
Daniel Wilhelm
Right row:
Katie Wilhelm,
Laura Younger

not pictured: Alex Brooks, Kathryn Byron

CONTENTS

1. Relationships

FRIENDS

God bless the friends
Who grace my life.

The ones who are bedrock,
Solid and steadfast,
And there forever.

The ones who are skyrockets,
Flashing suddenly into my life,
Bright and exciting,
But quickly gone.

The ones who are butterflies,
Soft and quiet,
Who enchant me briefly
And then fly on,
Leaving me with
A fond smile and
A heart full of memories.
Thank God for friends.

Sandra E. McBride

BOYFRIEND

Help me to have confidence
When he asks me to be something I'm not.
I don't want to fight
Or say he's not right,
But my self is the best thing I've got.

Help me to be wise and brave
When he asks me to change who I am
For what he doesn't get
Is that he must respect
My right to be all that I can.

Celia Straus

GUARD ME FROM
DESTRUCTIVE THOUGHTS

God, help me be warm and friendly;
　Let Your love be seen in me —
For traits I see in others,
　They may also see in me.

And guard me from destructive thoughts
　So others I don't condemn —
For when I think they're judging me . . .
　I'm really judging them.

Denise A. DeWald

SCHOOL PALS

Beneath this mask
Of cool indifference
Below the superficial layer
Of icy aloofness
There is a person.
Me.
Struggling to get out.
But bound inside
By your bitter jeers
   mocking words
      and label of Weird.

On the surface
I feign sophistication,
Acting as though
I do not care
About your group experiences.
Reality:
The impact
Of your words
Is eating my insides
   drowning my mind
      murdering my youth.

You ostracize me
To build
Your own egos.

Why?

Sheryl Stone Clay, age 16

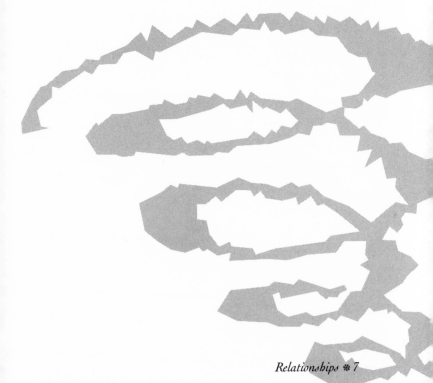

DELIVER US FROM
JUMPING TO CONCLUSIONS

Caution us, dear God, against fearing and hating all who talk and wear their hair, clothes, manners, and skin color "differently." How quickly we jump to conclusions. Help us spot value in all those we meet. For, O God, what opportunities we miss when we build fences to keep out "strangers" only to discover we've trapped ourselves behind a wall, too.

Margaret Anne Huffman
(1941–2000)

THE HARDEST PART IS PEOPLE

The hardest part is people.
So Lord, help me face them
without rancor or disappointment.
Help me see the pain behind their actions
rather than the malice;
the suffering rather than the rage.

And in myself, as I struggle
with the vise of my own desire —
give me the strength to quiet my heart,
to quicken my empathy, to act
in gratitude rather than need.

Remind me that the peace I find
in the slow track of seasons
or an uncurling fern frond,
is married to the despair I feel
in the face of nuclear war.

Remind me that each small bird shares atoms
with anthrax, with tetanus, with acid rain,
that each time I close my heart
to another, I add to the darkness;
Help me always follow kindness.

Let this be my prayer.

Karen Holden

NOBODY'S FRIEND

My name is Gossip. I have no respect for justice.

I maim without killing. I break hearts and ruin lives.

I am cunning and malicious and gather
   strength with age.

The more I am quoted the more I am believed.

My victims are helpless. They cannot protect themselves
   against me because I have no name and no face.

To track me down is impossible. The harder you try,
   the more elusive I become.

I am nobody's friend.

Once I tarnish a reputation, it is never the same.

I topple governments and wreck marriages.

I ruin careers and cause sleepless nights,
   heartaches, and indigestion.

I make innocent people cry in their pillows.

Even my name hisses. I am called Gossip.
  I make headlines and headaches.

Before you repeat a story, ask yourself: Is it true?
  Is it harmless? Is it necessary?

If it isn't, don't repeat it.

Author unknown

I WAS WRONG — FORGIVE ME

Lord,

help me to face the truth about myself.

Help me to hear my words as others hear them,

to see my face as others see me;

let me be honest enough to recognize my impatience
  and conceit;

let me recognize my anger and selfishness;

give me sufficient humility to accept my own weaknesses

for what they are.

Give me the grace — at least in your presence —

to say, "I was wrong — forgive me."

The Reverend Frank Topping

IN SPITE OF EVERYTHING

I keep my ideals,
because in spite of everything
I still believe that people
are really good at heart.

Anne Frank
(1929–1945)

IN THE END

In the end, nothing
we do or say
in this lifetime
will matter as much
as the way
we have loved
one another.

Daphne Rose Kingma

IT BEGINS AT HOME

Peace and war begin at home. If we truly want peace in the world, let us begin by loving one another in our own families. If we want to spread joy, we need for every family to have joy.

Mother Teresa
(1910–1997)

A BLESSING FOR FAMILY

May our family be blessed with comforts of the physical
    And riches of the spirit.
May our paths be lit with sunshine
    And sorrow ne'er darken our doors.
May our harvest be bountiful
    And our hearth ever welcoming.
May we celebrate together in times of joy
    And comfort one another in times of sorrow.
And mostly:
May we always stay together
    And share the laughter, the love, and the tears
        As only family can.

Danielle Brigante, age 19

HOW MUCH OUR WORDS MEAN

I often wonder if we realize how much our words
mean to those around us. While sharp, critical words
erect walls between people, words of encouragement
and appreciation build bridges, and do much to
strengthen relationships with family and friends.

The Reverend Dale Turner

REFLECTIONS ON RELATIONSHIPS

Some people come into our lives and quickly go.
Some stay for a while and leave footprints on our hearts.
And we are never, ever the same.
Author unknown

We all take different paths in life,
but no matter where we go,
we take a little of each other everywhere.
Tim McGraw

Smile if you want a smile from another face.
The Dalai Lama

When someone is acting difficult to love,
that usually means they are needing it terribly.
Margaret Anne Huffman
(1941–2000)

Maturity begins to grow when you can sense
your concern for others outweighing
your concern for yourself.
John MacNaughton

So long as you can sweeten another's pain,
life is not in vain.
Helen Keller
(1880–1968)

2. Comfort

DO NOT WORRY

Do not worry about your life,
what you will eat;
or about your body,
what you will wear.
Life is more than food,
and the body more than clothes.
Consider the ravens: they do not sow or reap,
they have no storeroom or barn;
yet God feeds them.

Luke 12:22–24 NIV.

FOOTPRINTS

One night a man had a dream. He dreamed he was walking along the beach with the Lord. Across the sky flashed scenes from his life. For each scene, he noticed two sets of footprints in the sand; one belonging to him, and the other to the Lord.

When the last scene of his life flashed before him, he looked back at the footprints in the sand. He noticed that many times along the path of his life there was only one set of footprints. He also noticed that it happened at the very lowest and saddest times in his life.

This really bothered him, and he questioned the Lord about it. "Lord, you said that once I decided to follow you, you would walk with me all the way. But I have noticed that during the most troublesome times in my life, there is only one set of footprints. I don't understand why, when I needed you most, you would leave me?"

The Lord replied, "My precious, precious child, I love you and I would never leave you. During your times of trial and suffering, when you see only one set of footprints, it was then that I carried you."

Mary Stevenson
(1922–1999)

I'M NEVER ALONE

I wonder if I'll make it
I wonder if I'll succeed
I wonder if I'll be accepted
just for being me.

When life gets tough
or when it's fun
I'll thank God
for all he's done —
for making it okay to mess up sometimes,
for helping me face the unknown,
for showing me there is always hope,
and that I'm never alone.

Ally Rakoczy, age 13

A VOICE INSIDE OF ME

So far in my life
I've had many ups and downs.
But a voice from inside keeps saying,
"I will take care of you
and everything will be alright."

When I've been hurt by others
'cause of what they say,
the voice says again,
"I will take care of you
and everything will be alright."

And when all my friends leave me,
the voice repeats,
"I will take care of you
and everything will be alright."

No matter what happens to me
I know I will be taken care of
and everything will be alright.

And when I forget,
I know the voice inside of me is God
and He will say again, "I will take care
of you and everything will be alright."

Suzanne Bertrand, age 13

YOU ARE NOT ALONE

I wrote this for anyone, boy or girl, who has had to see that pained look in your mother's eyes as she begs in vain for you to "take just one more bite" or whose mother leaves the unfinished half of chicken breast on your plate hoping that you will "pick at it." This is for all those who ever wished that they could just enjoy one meal without feeling as if they have failed themselves. For anyone who stands in front of the mirror, pinching and poking at hated curves and bumps. For anyone who wishes fervently that all traces of fat would just disappear, leaving you thin. I want you to know you are not alone.

Author unknown

DIALOGUE OF PRAYER

Me: I pray to be the same height as the other girls. I am too tall.

God: I pray you realize your gift of height, and always walk with head held high.

Me: I pray to be more practical. I am a daydreamer, a wishful thinker.

God: I pray you remember, without a wish, without a dream, you would be lost.

Me: I pray to become perfect. I am frustrated, and fearful.

God: I pray you understand growth comes when you allow yourself to be frustrated, to be scared.

Me: I pray to be independent—come and go as I please. I am too restricted.

God: I pray you recognize the love of family that keeps you safe.

Me: I pray to be accepting of myself.

God: I pray you learn to accept yourself.

Nadia Kourehdar, age 14

PRESSURE

There is pressure surrounding me,
pressure to do well,
and pressure to live up to other people's expectations.
Sometimes, I can't handle it.
I feel like a bird trying to fly with a broken wing,
and every time I get off the ground,
someone shoots me down.

But when I turn to God,
my problems are erased,
he lifts the pain and pressure off of me,
and I take refuge in his embrace.

Katie Bonacini, age 13

WHY ME?

If you've had problems, difficulties, or illness in your life (and who hasn't?), sometime along the way you've probably asked the question "Why me?" Maybe the answer you got was that difficulties in life are "learning experiences." Did you believe it?

No one is immune to tragedy, bad luck, or ill fate. But everyone can learn to stand strong against hardship and adversity. Don't let depression get the best of you. You can survive physically, emotionally, and spiritually.

Sometimes problems may even be gifts in disguise. Have you ever heard the story about the man whose only riches were his beloved son and his twenty stallions?

One night, the corral gate was left open, and the man's twenty stallions ran away into the hills. The man wept and cursed his bad luck. The next morning, he awoke to find that his twenty stallions had returned, each with a wild mare. "This is very good, for now I have forty horses," he said. But his beloved son was thrown while trying to ride one of the wild mares, and he broke his leg in the accident. "How horrible!" cried the man. "My son is in such pain. This is very bad!" That evening, a hundred of the king's soldiers swept through the village and gathered all the able-bodied young men to fight a war far away. The man's son wasn't taken because of his broken leg. The man laughed and said to his son, "Perhaps, in this case, a broken leg is good."

Sometimes how you think about an event and how you react to it are more important than the event itself. If something happens that you don't like, you can *choose* how to deal with it. If you look at your misfortunes as learning experiences and life challenges that you can survive and overcome, you'll grow stronger. Ask yourself, "How can I make this work *for* me instead of *against* me?" Tell yourself you won't just be a victim of your circumstances—you'll accept them, deal with them . . . and rise above them.

Bev Cobain

(The above story was excerpted from the book When Nothing Matters Anymore: A Survival Guide for Depressed Teens *by Bev Cobain, cousin of rock star Kurt Cobain, who committed suicide in 1994 at the age of 27.)*

REFLECTIONS ON PAIN AND LOSS

Pain is a part of being alive,
and we need to learn that.
Pain does not last forever,
nor is it necessarily unbearable,
and we need to be taught that.
Rabbi Harold Kushner

If we had no winter,
the spring would not be so pleasant;
if we did not sometimes taste of adversity,
prosperity would not be so welcome.
Anne Bradstreet
(1612–1672)

When one door closes another door opens;
but we often look so longingly
and so regretfully upon the door that closed,
that we fail to see the one that has opened for us.
Helen Keller
(1880–1968)

Some people think it's holding on that makes one strong.
Sometimes it's letting go.
Sylvia Robinson

ANGEL EMBRACE

There are angels who sit quietly
and whisper when we need comfort.
There are those who breathe life into us
when we are breathless.

There are angels who fill us with gracious support
when our souls become fragile,
and those who kiss us good night for a peaceful slumber.

There are angels who touch us with sacred laughter
when tears become a burden.
There are those who wrap their wings around us
and rock us until the ache in our heart disappears.

There are angels who can send us flying with wonder
when our hope begins to fade,
and those who devote everything to give us
everlasting peace in heaven.

Lori Eberhardy

DIVORCE
(A Prayer of Perseverance)

Dear God, do you see me?
My boat sails gently.
I am peaceful.
Love surrounds me.

Dear God, do you see me?
The waters around me roughen.
I am in the midst of their fighting.
The two people that brought me here
and stood by my side
have turned against each other.

Dear God, do you see me?
Waves increase as I am tossed about.
With the realization that their love
for me is eternal,
but for each other is not.

Dear God, do you see me?
I am caught between ocean and shore.
My world separates into two.
My mother stands alone. My father stands alone.

Dear God, do you see me?
Through the roughness of the storm,
my eyes become clear.
My breathing slows.
Love still surrounds me.

Dear God, do you see me?
I am peaceful once again.
I am okay . . . you've always seen me.

Dear God, thank you.

Nadia Kourehdar, age 14

I BELIEVE IN GOD

I believe in the sun even when
    it does not shine.
I believe in love even when
    I do not feel it.
I believe in God even when
    he is silent.

Author unknown

*(Inscription on a cellar wall in Cologne, Germany,
where Jews hid from Nazis during World War II)*

WORDS OF COMFORT

The will of God can never lead
where the grace of God cannot keep you.
Author unknown

New beginnings start as the seed of a flower does,
buried, unseen,
but destined to bloom.
Corrine De Winter

Character cannot be developed in ease and quiet.
Only through experience of trial and suffering
can the soul be strengthened,
ambition inspired, and success achieved.
Helen Keller
(1880–1968)

In the midst of winter,
I found there was within me
an invincible summer.
Albert Camus
(1913–1960)

Our greatest glory is not in never falling,
but in rising every time we fall.
Confucius
(551–479 B.C.E.)

3. Encouragement

CHRYSALIS

Throughout life
you will learn
that sorrow will not remain.
You will see that it is
like a butterfly
emerging
from its cocoon
to make way
for greater things.

Corrine De Winter

WHO AM I NOW?

O God,
who am I now?
Once, I was secure in familiar territory,
in my sense of belonging,
unquestioning of the norms of my culture,
the assumptions built into my language,
the values shared by my society.
But now you have called me out and away from home
and I do not know where you are leading.
I am empty, unsure, uncomfortable.
I have only a beckoning star to follow.

Journeying God,
pitch your tent with mine
so that I may not become deterred
by hardship, strangeness, doubt.
Show me the movement I must make
toward a wealth not dependent on possessions
toward a wisdom not based on books
toward a strength not bolstered by might
toward a God not confined to heaven
but scandalously earthed, poor, unrecognized . . .
Help me find myself
as I walk in others' shoes.

Kate Compston

DO NOT BE AFRAID . . .

To fear—

> When you face your fears,
> you will find your courage.

To fail—

> From your failures, you will learn to succeed.

To fall—

> Your victory is in rising from the fall.

To stand alone—

> If you stand up for what you know
> in your heart is right,
> you will never stand alone.

To fly—

> Your faith will carry you as high as your dreams.

Sandra E. McBride

COURAGE

God,
give me the power
to reveal to others what
I feel;
and when my heart is
far too weak,
unlock my heart and
let it speak!

Thomas L. Reid

THE WORK OF PEACE

Give us courage, O Lord, to stand up and be counted,
to stand up for those who cannot stand up for
    themselves,
to stand up for ourselves when it is needful for us
    to do so.
Let us fear nothing more than we fear you.
Let us love nothing more than we love you,
for thus we shall fear nothing also . . .
Let us seek no other peace but the peace which is
    yours,
and make us its instruments,
opening our eyes and our ears and our hearts,
so that we should know always what work of peace
we may do for you.

Alan Paton
(1903–1988)

MAKE A PEARL

Most of us can afford to take a lesson from the oyster. The most extraordinary thing about the oyster is this. Irritations get into his shell. He does not like them; he tries to get rid of them. But when he cannot get rid of them he settles down to make of them one of the most beautiful things in the world. He uses the irritation to do the loveliest thing that an oyster ever has a chance to do. If there are irritations in our lives today, there is only one prescription: make a pearl. It may have to be a pearl of patience, but, anyhow, make a pearl. And it takes faith and love to do it.

Harry Emerson Fosdick
(1878–1969)

UNENDING LOVE

We are loved
by an unending love.
We are embraced
by arms that find us
even when
we are hidden from ourselves.
We are touched
by fingers that soothe us
even when
we are too proud for soothing.
We are counseled
by voices that guide us
even when
we are too embittered to hear.
We are loved
by an unending love.

We are supported
by hands that uplift us
even in
the midst of a fall.
We are urged on
by eyes that meet us
even when
we are too weak for meeting.
We are loved
by an unending love.
Embraced, touched, soothed, and counseled . . .
ours are the arms,
the fingers, the voices;
ours are the hands,
the eyes, the smiles;
We are loved
by an unending love.

Rabbi Rami M. Shapiro

REJOICE

And we rejoice in the hope of the glory of God.
Not only so, but we also rejoice in our sufferings,
because we know that suffering produces perseverance;
perseverance, character;
and character, hope.

Romans 5:2–4 NIV.

✱ ✱ ✱ ✱ ✱

WORDS OF ENCOURAGEMENT

The fishermen know that the sea is dangerous
and the storm terrible, but they have never found
these dangers sufficient reason for remaining ashore.
Vincent van Gogh
(1853–1890)

You miss 100 percent of the shots you never take.
Wayne Gretzky

The way I see it, if you want the rainbow,
you gotta put up with the rain.
Dolly Parton

Keep your face to the sunshine
and you cannot see the shadow.
Helen Keller
(1880–1968)

4. Praise and Gratitude

THE A–Z PRAYER

Think of something or someone for each letter of the alphabet. It could be a person, or a thing, or a concept that makes you feel happy or peaceful. For example, A could be Alex, applesauce, action . . . or any number of words. Try this when you want a lift. You'll be surprised at how your word strings change each time. Here's just one example:

Angels
    Beauty
        Color
            Dreams
              Energy
                Flying
                Goodness
                Hope
                Inspiration
                Justice
              Kindness
            Love
          Music
        Nature
      Oranges

Peace
Quickness
Running
Spring
Traveling
Understanding
Very good friends
Wonder
eXcitement
Yesterday
Zebras

Author unknown

FOR ALL THINGS

For all things bright and beautiful,
For all things dark and mysterious and lovely,
For all things green and growing and strong,
For all things weak and struggling to push life up
    through rocky earth,
For all human faces, hearts, minds, and hands which
    surround us,
And for all nonhuman minds and hearts, paws and
    claws, fins and wings,
For this Life and the life of this world,
For all that you have laid before us, O God,
We lay our thankful hearts before you.

Gail A. Ricciuti

MOTHER NATURE'S SCHOOL
(A Prayer of Gratitude)

I learned of respect from the ocean—powerful waves,
    yet soothing sound.

I learned of peace from clouds—their slow movement,
    never showing agitation.

I learned of music from birds—repetitive melody and
    rhythmic expression.

I learned of anger from thunder—it soon passes.

I learned the power of silence—from the stillness
    of air.

I learned of distress, from floods, fires, and
    earthquakes—how lives can change in an instant.

I learned of joy from springtime—new life, sprouting
    grass, blossoms.

Mother Nature, you've helped my spirit grow.

I like your school.

Amen.

Nadia Kourehdar, age 14

MOST RICHLY BLESSED

I asked God for strength, that I might achieve;
I was made weak, that I might learn humbly to obey.
I asked for health, that I might do greater things;
I was given infirmity, that I might do better things.
I asked for power, that I might have the praise of men;
I was given weakness, that I might feel the need of
  God.
I asked for all things, that I might enjoy life;
I was given life, that I might enjoy all things.
I got nothing I asked for
but everything I had hoped for;
Almost despite myself, my unspoken prayers were
  answered.
I am, among all men, most richly blessed.

Author unknown

*(These words were found on the body of a soldier
killed in the Civil War.)*

THIS I KNOW

My body is paralyzed.
By God's strength someday I will be free.
When that day comes I will be filled with joy.
   This I know.
I haven't walked from the day I was born,
On the warm backs of my parents and
brothers and sisters
I can go anywhere.
   This I know.
I am unable to speak.
I cannot speak gossip
Or speak harsh words.
   This I know.
In the midst of sorrow and pain
There is joy and happiness.
In the midst of this, I am alive.
   This I know.

Kumi Hayashi

GOD OF JOY

God of joy,
I glimpsed you
in broad daylight.

A robe of light
enfolded the tree
without memory of the cross.

Your crystal footsteps
descended the staircase
of the spring.

The sky smiled;
flower and pebble
shared good company.

Everything was a divine
language.
Each wing a journey

toward all light,
God of Joy.
The world is on fire.

Jorge Carrera Andrade
Translated by Steven Ford Brown

GOD, THANK YOU
FOR EVERYTHING

Dear God,

Sometimes I believe I forget to thank you. You have given me so many great things, and I think I sometimes take advantage of that. So now I want to thank you for my family, friends, and the food I have. I would also like to pray for those who are less fortunate than I am—those who haven't been blessed with the many things I have. I ask you to help so that I will have the courage to reach out to the outcasts that are too often ridiculed. I try to be friends with everyone, but it is not always easy. God, thank you for everything. Amen.

Rachel E. Cox, age 12

NATURAL HIGHS

Falling in love.

Laughing so hard your face hurts.

A hot shower.

No lines at the grocery store.

A special glance.

Getting mail.

Taking a drive on a pretty road.

Hearing your favorite song on the radio.

Lying in bed listening to the rain outside.

Hot towels out of the dryer.

A long-distance phone call.

A bubble bath.

Giggling.

A good conversation.

The beach.

Finding a $20 bill in your coat from last winter.

Laughing at yourself.

Running through sprinklers.

Laughing for absolutely no reason at all.

Having someone tell you that you are beautiful.

Laughing at an inside joke.

Friends.

Accidentally overhearing someone saying something
   nice about you.

Waking up and realizing you still have a few hours left
to sleep.

Your first kiss.

Making new friends and spending time with old ones.

Playing with a puppy.

Late night talks with your roommate that keep you
from sleeping.

Sweet dreams.

Hot chocolate.

Road trips with friends.

Swinging on swings.

Watching a good movie cuddled up on the couch with
someone you love.

Song lyrics printed inside your new CD so that you
can sing along and not feel stupid.

Going to a really good concert.

Getting butterflies in your stomach every time you see
that one person.

Making eye contact with a cute stranger.

Winning a really competitive game.

Making chocolate chip cookies!

Spending time with close friends.

Holding hands with someone you care about.

Discovering love is unconditional and stronger
than time.

Riding the best roller coasters over and over.

Hugging the person you love.

Watching the sunrise.

Getting out of bed every morning and thanking God
for another beautiful day.

Author unknown

I MAY NEVER SEE TOMORROW

I may never see tomorrow,
there's no guarantee,
and things that happened yesterday
belong to history.

I can't predict the future,
I can't change the past,
I have just the present memories
to treat as my last.

I must use this moment wisely,
for soon it will pass away,
and be lost forever
as a part of yesterday.

I must exercise compassion,
help the fallen to their feet,
be a friend unto the friendless,
make their life complete.

The unkind things I do today,
may never be undone,
and friendships that I fail to win,
may never more be won.

I may not have another chance
on bended knees to pray,
and I thank God with a humble heart
for giving me this day!

I may never see tomorrow,
but this moment is my own.
It's mine to use or cast aside:
the choice is mine, alone.

I have just this precious moment
in the sunlight of today,
where the dawning of tomorrow
meets the dusk of yesterday.

George L. Nolan

5. Love, Kindness, and Forgiveness

THOUGHTS ON LOVE

Love is life. . . . And if you miss love, you miss life.
Leo Buscaglia
(1924–1998)

None of us has the power to make someone else love us.
But we all have the power to give away love,
to love other people. And if we do so,
we change the kind of person we are,
and we change the kind of world we live in.
Rabbi Harold Kushner

What I know for sure is that your life is a mulitpart series
of all your experiences—and each experience is created by
your thoughts, intentions, and actions, to teach you what
you most need to know. Your life is a journey of learning
to love yourself first and then extending that love to others
in every encounter.

Oprah Winfrey

Love does not consist in gazing at each other,
but in looking outward together in the same direction.
Antoine de Saint-Exupery
(1900–1994)

The conclusion is always the same:
love is the most powerful and still the most
unknown energy of the world.
Pierre Teilhard De Chardin
(1881–1955)

'Tis better to have loved and lost
than never to have loved at all.
Alfred, Lord Tennyson
(1809–1892)

LOVE IS PATIENT

Love is patient, love is kind.
It does not envy, it does not boast,
it is not proud. It is not rude,
it is not self-seeking,
it is not easily angered,
it keeps no record of wrongs.

Love does not delight in evil
but rejoices with the truth.
It always protects, always trusts,
always hopes, always perseveres.
Love never fails.

And now these three remain:
faith, hope and love.
But the greatest of these is love.

I Corinthians 13:4–8, 13 NIV.

IF YOU HAVE
A PARTICULAR FAITH

If you have a particular faith or religion,
that is good.
But you can survive without it
if you have love, compassion, and tolerance.
The clear proof of a person's love of God
is if that person genuinely shows
love to fellow human beings.

The Dalai Lama

❋ ❋ ❋ ❋ ❋

THE GOLDEN RULE

Buddhism

One should seek for others the happiness
one desires for himself.

Christianity

Do to others as you would have them do to you.

Hinduism

The true rule of life
is to guard and to do
by the things of others
as one would to his own.

Islam

No one of you is a believer
until he desires for his brother
that which he desires for himself.

Judaism

Do to no one what you would not want done to you.

BLESSINGS OF THE HEART

If you are poor,
live wisely.
If you have riches,
live wisely.
It is not your station in life
but your heart
that brings blessings.

The Buddha
(563–483 B.C.E.)

REFLECTIONS ON KINDNESS

We can do no great things,
only small things with great love.
Mother Teresa
(1910–1997)

My religion is very simple. My religion is kindness.
The Dalai Lama

Each and every act of kindness done
by anyone anywhere
resonates out into the world and somehow,
mysteriously, invisibly, and perfectly,
touches us all.
Mary Jane Ryan

Kindness is a language which the deaf
can hear and the blind can read.
Mark Twain
(1835–1910)

The kindest word in all the world
is the unkind word, unsaid.
Author unknown

Practice random kindness and senseless acts of beauty.
Anne Herbert

No act of kindness, however small, is ever wasted.
Aesop

LORD, OPEN OUR EYES

Lord, open our eyes,

That we may see you in our brothers and sisters.

Lord, open our ears,

That we may hear the cries of the hungry, the cold,

the frightened, the oppressed.

Lord, open our hearts,

That we may love each other as you love us.

Renew in us your spirit,

Lord, free us and make us one.

Attributed to Mother Teresa
(1910–1997)

LET IT SPRING FROM LOVE

The thought manifests as the word;
The word manifests as the deed;
The deed develops into habit;
And habit hardens into character.
    So watch the thought and its ways with care,
And let it spring from love
Born out of concern for all beings.

The Buddha
(563–483 B.C.E.)

FORGIVENESS

Dear God, remember not only the men and women of goodwill but also those of ill will. But do not remember the suffering they have inflicted upon us—remember the fruits we brought, thanks to this suffering: our comradeship, our loyalty, our humility, the courage, the generosity, the greatness of heart which has grown out of this—and when they come to judgment, let all the fruits that we have borne be their forgiveness.

(The prayer of an unknown woman, found on a piece of wrapping paper in Ravensbruck concentration camp)

✳ ✳ ✳ ✳ ✳

THOUGHTS ON FORGIVENESS

He who cannot forgive others destroys
the bridge over which he himself must pass.
George Herbert
(1593–1633)

If you haven't forgiven yourself something,
how can you forgive others?
Dolores Huerta

When a deep injury is done to us,
we never recover until we forgive.
Alan Paton
(1903–1988)

Those you do not forgive you fear.
And no one reaches love with fear beside him.
From A Course in Miracles

Forgive the past and let it go, for it *is* gone.
From A Course in Miracles

MAY I REACH OUT

May I reach out to someone who needs me
  Someone who's lonely
  Someone who's shy
  Someone who's quiet when others are talking
  Someone whose smile
  Is hiding a cry.

May I make friends with someone who needs me
  Someone who's left out
  Someone who's new
  Someone who's searching for a place to fit in
  Someone who's wanting
  Someone like me, too.

Celia Straus

6. Individuality

REFLECTIONS ON INDIVIDUALITY

Embrace your uniqueness.
Time is much too short
to be living someone else's life.
Kobi Yamada

In the silence of the self
it is only my own voice
I must answer to.
Corrine De Winter

I didn't belong as a kid,
and that always bothered me.
If only I'd known that one day
my differentness would be an asset,
then my early life would have been much easier.
Bette Midler

Until you make peace with who you are,
you'll never be content with what you have.
Doris Mortman

We all matter. Every one of us has
an essential contribution to make, and we can do so only
by taking the risk of being uniquely our own selves.
Carol S. Pearson

Somewhere someone is looking
for exactly what you have to offer.
Louise L. Hay

Do not follow where the path may lead.
Go instead where there is no path,
and leave a trail.
Author unknown

Go confidently in the direction of your dreams!
Live the life you've imagined.
Henry David Thoreau
(1817–1862)

Do not wish to be anything
but what you are,
and try to be that perfectly.
Saint Francis De Sales
(1567–1622)

THE UNIQUENESS OF YOU

When
God
made
you
there
was
silence
in
heaven
for
five
minutes.
Then
God
said:
"How come I never thought of that before?"

Father Ralph Wright

WHOLE

You are a light unto yourself.
You are beauty
Which walks in grace.
You are whole
Even when it feels
As though you are broken.
You are loved
Even when you feel
So very small
In the wide open universe.

You are a light unto yourself.

Corrine De Winter

THE VOICE

There is a voice inside of you
That whispers all day long,
"I feel that this is right for me,
I know that this is wrong."
No teacher, preacher, parents, friend
Or wise man can decide
What's right for you—just listen to
The voice that speaks inside.

Shel Silverstein
(1932–1999)

THOUGHTS TO INSPIRE

The future belongs to those who believe
in the beauty of their dreams.
Eleanor Roosevelt
(1884–1962)

It's a funny thing about life;
if you refuse to accept anything but the best,
you very often get it.
Somerset Maugham
(1874–1965)

Even if I knew that tomorrow
the world would go to pieces,
I would still plant my apple tree.
Martin Luther
(1483–1546)

Only put off until tomorrow
what you are willing
to die having left undone.
Pablo Picasso
(1881–1973)

People forget how fast you did a job —
but they remember how well you did it.
Howard W. Newton

"I can't do it" never yet accomplished anything;
"I will try" has performed wonders.
George P. Burnham

Believe that life is worth living,
and your belief will help create the fact.
William James
(1842–1910)

I am particularly fond of the little groves of oak trees.
I love to look at them,
because they endure the wintry storm
and the summer's heat,
and—not unlike ourselves—seem to flourish by them.
Sitting Bull
(1831–1890)

Creativity is God's gift to you.
What you do with it is your gift to God.
Bob Moawad

Start small
Dream big
Live large
Jana Stanfield

YOUR TALENT

Every person on this earth has a natural talent. You've got to find yours and then figure out a way to make a living using it. That's the key to happiness in your professional life. Don't let anybody else tell you what to do. You figure it out. . . .

Once you figure out your talent, then you have to do the other very difficult thing in life. And that's to live honorably. You have to do what you say you are going to do. It's as simple as that. . . . If you live by that code, you will accomplish what you want to accomplish. . . .

There is an order to the universe. The sun goes up, the sun goes down. The tide comes in, the tide goes out. The seasons change. There is also an order to your life.

Good things are going to happen; bad things are going to happen. There is nothing you can do to prevent those things. But, it's how you react to the good and to the bad that will make the difference at the end of your life.

When you look back from your deathbed to what your life was, it will all come down to how you handled the things that came your way. How you evaluated people, how you chose your mate, how you chose your friends. . . .

Be honorable. Find your talent. Work hard. And be true to yourself. Your life is waiting for you.

Bill O'Reilly

LET YOUR LIGHT SHINE

Our deepest fear is not that we are inadequate. It's
that we are powerful beyond measure. It is our light,
not our darkness, that most frightens us. We ask
ourselves, Who am I to be brilliant, gorgeous, talented,
and fabulous?

Actually, who are you not to be? You are a child
of God. Your playing small doesn't serve the world.
We were born to make manifest the glory of God
that is within us.

It's not just in some of us, it's in everyone. As we
let our own light shine, we unconsciously give
other people permission to do the same.

As we are liberated from our own fear, our
presence automatically liberates others.

Marianne Williamson

ISN'T IT AMAZING?

I am just so thankful to God for everything He's done for me, as well as for others. Even when things are bad, He's stood next to me and things are a little less prone to becoming blown out of proportion by my emotions. . . . You know, I wonder what God is going to do with my life. Like my purpose. Some people become missionaries and things, but what about me? What does God have in store for me? Where do my talents and gifts lie? For now, I'll just take it day by day. I'm confident that I'll know someday. Maybe I'll look back at my life and think "Oh, so that was it!" Isn't it amazing, this plan we're a part of? . . .

Cassie Bernall
(1981–1999)

(An excerpt from a letter Cassie Bernall wrote about a year before she died in the Columbine shooting)

WHAT IS GOD'S PLAN FOR ME?

Sometimes,
I lie awake late at night,
not reading or listening to music,
but just thinking about my day,
whether sorrowful, joyful, or just ok.
And I wonder,
what is God's plan for me?
This is such a critical point in my life,
between childhood and adulthood,
a time when emotions rage,
pressures surround,
and change is in every breath we take.
I am moving on to another school,
making new friends,
and eventually, I'll be on my own,
in a world that can be harsh, cold, cruel,
but also beautiful, enchanting, and perfect.
At times we can be discouraged from our goals,
or they could be in open reach,
but through it all,
I wonder,
What is God's plan for me?

Katie Bonacini, age 13

✻ ✻ ✻ ✻ ✻

THOUGHTS ON
MAKING A DIFFERENCE

You must be the change
you wish to see in the world.
Mahatma Gandhi
(1869–1948)

One of the deepest secrets of life
is that all that is really worth doing
is what we do for others.
Lewis Carroll
(1832–1898)

To accomplish great things,
we must not only act,
but also dream,
not only plan,
but also believe.
Anatole France
(1844–1924)

How wonderful it is
that nobody need wait a single moment
before starting to improve the world.
Anne Frank
(1929–1945)

OUR WINGS

Throughout life
we search for our wings,
but find beauty
at every level,
remembering that
even winged creatures
begin their journey on earth.

Corrine De Winter

UNTIL THE END

In the end
and until the end
I start over each day.

I am beginning
again and again
to see
ever more clearly
by the light of
my own smile.

Kate Robinson

NO REGRETS

Finish every day and be done with it. You have done what you could. Some blunders and absurdities no doubt crept in; forget them as soon as you can. Tomorrow is a new day; begin it well and serenely and with too high a spirit to be encumbered with your old nonsense.

This day is all that is good and fair. It is too dear with its hopes and invitations to waste a moment on the yesterdays.

Author unknown

BE HERE NOW

Don't think about the future.
Just be here now.

Don't think about the past.
Just be here now.

Bhagavan Das responding to a question by Ram Dass

IF I HAD MY LIFE TO LIVE OVER

If I had my life to live over,
    I'd dare to make more mistakes next time.
I'd relax, I would limber up.
I would be sillier than I have been this trip.
I would take fewer things seriously.
I would take more chances.
I would climb more mountains
    and swim more rivers.
I would eat more ice cream and less beans.
I would perhaps have more actual troubles,
    but I'd have fewer imaginary ones.
You see, I'm one of those people
    who lives sensibly and sanely
    hour after hour, day after day.
Oh, I've had my moments,
    and if I had it to do over again,
    I'd have more of them.

In fact, I'd try to have nothing else.
Just moments, one after another,
   instead of living so many years
   ahead of each day.

I've been one of those persons who never
   goes anywhere without a thermometer,
   a hot water bottle, a raincoat and
   a parachute.
If I had to do it again,
   I would travel lighter than I have.

If I had my life to live over,
   I would start barefoot earlier in the spring
   and stay that way later in the fall.
I would go to more dances.
I would ride more merry-go-rounds.
I would pick more daisies.

Nadine Stair

I HOPE YOU DANCE

I hope you never lose your sense of wonder
You get your fill to eat but always keep that hunger
May you never take one single breath for granted
God forbid love ever leave you empty-handed
I hope you still feel small
when you stand beside the ocean
Whenever one door closes I hope one more opens
Promise me that you'll give faith a fighting chance
And when you get the choice to sit it out or dance
I hope you dance . . . I hope you dance

Mark Sanders and Tia Sillers

7. Tolerance

✳ ✳ ✳ ✳ ✳

THOUGHTS ON THE WORLD

Love is the medicine
for the sickness of the world.
Karl Augustus Menninger
(1893–1990)

It's not enough to have lived.
We should be determined to live for something.
May I suggest that it be creating joy for others,
sharing what we have
for the betterment of personkind,
bringing hope to the lost and love to the lonely.
Leo Buscaglia
(1924–1998)

In order to achieve genuine,
lasting world peace based on compassion,
we need a sense of universal responsibility.
First, we have to try inner disarmament—
reducing our own anger and hatred
while increasing mutual trust
and human affection.
The Dalai Lama

What we do for ourselves dies with us.
What we do for others and the world
remains and is immortal.
Albert Pine

Mental sunshine will cause the flowers
of peace, happiness, and prosperity
to grow upon the face of the Earth.
Be a creator of mental sunshine.
Graffiti on a wall in Berkeley, California

HATE TO UNITE

In remembrance of the American tragedy, September 11, 2001

Our nation has united,
but look at what it took.
A national tragedy,
crisis and death.
Tears fallen
and loved ones lost.
This is what it took for hands
to be reached out
and then finally held.
To get us to unify,
to take the time to stop
and think of each other.

Hatred from others
brought us to one another.

Leah Sell, age 15

THE SACRIFICE OF
HALOS AND WINGS

The curtain falls and the world fades to black.
We pray to be taken from this place and to be put
    somewhere new.
A better place, a safe place.
The darkness echoes through our minds
    showing no mercy, and
it resonates in our souls leaving us empty.

As they began calling out the names of those who were lost,
God was calling out the names of those who were saved.
He beckons us to sift through the ashes and understand
we have all been brought together by circumstance,
but we will remain together by the grace of love.

This is where the journey begins and
in the silence God is working miracles.
We must be quiet, be still, and listen, and find a way
to make all of this fit into our world.

You may wonder if God can hear you cry.
He promises that the sun will dry your tears.
You may wonder if God knows your pain.
He promises that the rain will wash you clean.
It's time to close the door against this cold wind,
and as the rays of light peer through the clouds,
I invite you to embrace the sun.

This journey holds the secret to salvation.
When you see a rainbow in the distance remember that
it is the hope in your heart that will sustain you
and the faith in your soul that will set you free.

Lori Eberhardy

A RESPONSE TO THE
HOLOCAUST MUSEUM

Amid this twirling mobile of darkened suns,
   these neglected beds of dying lilies
release bitter scents from their crushed petals;
I am at a loss:
   about myself
   and everything else.
There are no words for this suffering;
no futile description of mine
   can cast a reflection worthy of their
broken eyes, shattered hearts, bodies, lives.
My removed compassion can build no wings
able to carry them from their pain;
   one person cannot overcome
all that darkness,
and certainly not I, merely a girl
   with plastered-paper wings ripped on the edges.

But lighting a candle
   in remembrance,
I know they have already been freed,
and are soaring
   above this murky sphere,
      guided by the white light
which glows in the desperate promise
of a girl who vows
   to never let it
happen again.

Caitlin R. Woolsey, age 16

COMBINATIONS

There is a combination for everything—
the way I wear my hair,
and you yours,
my squint
and your wide-open stare.
The combination
of words put to paper,
the combination
of words that never appear.

The Universe
combines us
and we commingle with the stars—
the way a comet passes its years
out there,
the way we pass ours
here.

Julia Older

STOPPING BY A CANDY SHELF

If only
the people of the world
could keep
their true separate flavors
and hold tight to each other
the way
Life Savers do.

Ida Fasel

HOLY WARS

Each day people fight.
They say their god is the real god.
Each group reads from their holy book
while their children suffer and die.

Long ago this land was
filled with peace and wisdom.
When will they stop,
the endless wars,
the "holy" wars —
to God I ask,
What do you think?

For all the children, Israeli and Palestinian,
who have needlessly died,
because they were in the wrong place
at the wrong time.
May we remember them
forever.

Ashley M. Payne, age 14

WHY ALL THE FIGHTING?

O God, the stars above shine with all your glory
and the flowers below glow with color.
But why all the fighting,
The wars, the anger?
I just want to paint your joy . . .
To paint the shade of green on each blade of grass,
or the silkiness of hair on the cat's back.
Please shine your light in my path. Amen.

Gemma McKean, age 12

WE ARE THE
CHILDREN OF THE FUTURE

We are the children of the future.
We fight no wars.
We pollute no seas.
Let us lead the way.

We kill no people.
We cut down no forests.
Let us lead the way, Lord.

Trevor Smith, age 13

PRAYER FOR HUMANITY

I pray that we learn to love more and demand less—
so that our love for one another will be our
ever-present reality and consciousness.

I pray that we experience our common humanity
and that we understand that all of us are more alike
than different.

I pray that I realize that my life won't work well unless
your life works well and that our lives on this planet
are deeply intertwined.

I pray that we learn that we have one world—
and that we no longer separate ourselves in the name
of national boundary lines.

I pray that we learn to disagree without throwing each
other out of our hearts—and not keep ourselves upset
over our differences.

I pray that we learn to forgive, for our own sake—
for a heart hardened with hatred is too heavy to carry.

I pray that we settle arguments in nonviolent ways —
that we learn to listen to one another and truly hear,
so that all arms become obsolete.

I pray that we act less impulsively — so that love and
wisdom may guide our actions.

I pray that we learn to experience the beauty in
ourselves and each other — and that we feel deep
appreciation for the good things we have.

I pray that we hear the message that God is love —
so that we no longer separate ourselves in the name
of religion.

I pray that we open our hearts and learn to live
together on this globe — so that we find our great
birthright of a loving life.

Ken Keyes, Jr.
(1921–1995)

I WONDER

As the voices of my mother's parents blend together
in a song of prayer,
As the Friday night candles burn after the blessing
over the wine,
As my hand touches the challah and a prayer is said,
I wonder. . . .

Is this God's chosen faith?
Is this where I belong?

As I listen to the Persian language spoken often
in my father's house,
As I gaze at the old Koran gathering dust on the table,
As I remember the smell and feel of the mosque,
I wonder. . . .

Is this God's chosen faith?
Is this where I belong?

As my friend laughs with me, I see a golden
cross dangling from her neck,
As I smell the freshly cut Christmas tree,
standing tall inside her home,
As every Sunday, attending church,
she worships her God,
I wonder. . . .

Is this God's chosen faith?
Is this where I belong?

I wonder. . . .
Perhaps there is no chosen faith.
Perhaps I "belong" when I realize no matter
what faith I choose,
God exists everywhere, equally, forever.
I wonder. . . .

Nadia Kourehdar, age 14

IF ONLY

If only we saw
What our eyes don't see
If only we heard
What our ears don't hear
If only we could walk
The steps unstepped
Just maybe
We'd wake up one day
To find ourselves
Someplace unsaid
Somewhere never heard of
Or ever revealed
In the midst of all eternity
If only . . .

Lia Nuno, age 16

REASON FOR HOPE

Question asked to Jane Goodall: *You mention four reasons for hope—the human brain, resilience, youth, and a collective power. Please explain more about collective power.*

It's the indomitable human spirit in each one of us. Each one of us makes a difference. And we all think we are insignificant since there are six billion of us and that the little bits that we do don't actually make any difference—turning off the lights, walking rather than taking the car. It's very hard to think that what I do really makes a difference, and it wouldn't if it were just me. So it's the collective power of everyone taking the responsibility. . . . Everyone can make that difference.

Jane Goodall

IF THERE IS LIGHT
IN THE SOUL

If there is light in the soul,
There will be beauty in the person.
If there is beauty in the person,
There will be harmony in the home.
If there is harmony in the home,
There will be order in the nation.
If there is order in the nation,
There will be peace in the world.

Chinese proverb

REFLECTIONS ON TOLERANCE

O God, help us not to despise or oppose
what we do not understand.
William Penn
(1644–1718)

O Great Spirit, help me never to judge another
until I have walked two weeks in his moccasins.
Sioux prayer

Racism is a product of fear and ignorance.
The world is richer for the mixture
of different types of people — live and let live — remove fear.
Gavin Rossdale

We have to adopt a wider perspective,
and always find common things between
the people of north, east, south, and west.
Conflict comes from the basis of differences.
The Dalai Lama

In high school I have learned to choose my friends
by their character and my socks by their color.
Kyle Sandburg, age 18

There isn't even enough time for love,
so what does that leave for hate?
Bill Copeland

8. Nightfall

ON GOING TO BED

As my head rests on my pillow
Let my soul rest in your mercy.

As my limbs relax on my mattress,
Let my soul relax in your peace.

As my body finds warmth beneath the blankets,
Let my soul find warmth in your love.

As my mind is filled with dreams,
Let my soul be filled with visions of heaven.

Johann Freylinghausen
(1670–1739)

AS PEOPLE TURN TO SLEEP

Dear God, as people turn to sleep,
please bless all those who
cannot sleep tonight.
Comfort those who are sad.
Forgive those who have done wrong.
Calm those who are worried.
Help those who are in pain.
And grant Your peace
to every troubled heart.

Author unknown

TO DREAM

The sun has just now set in the horizon,
I climb into my bed like a weary traveler.
Then, as is part of my routine, I close my eyes,
ready to dream, putting myself into God's hands.

Now,
My perils have turned to nothingness,
and my ideas swarm like bees
surrounding their hives.

My imagination sails as smoothly and effortlessly
as a sailboat,
for I leave my earthly body behind,
to be cradled by my lord.

My soul is set free!

This is my time to be myself,
and fly, like the wind,
to imaginary places
worlds beyond our own earth's sky.

Into God's whirlpool I go,
spun by his own angels,
never to return the same again.

Katie Bonacini, age 13

SACREDNESS

Some nights, stay up till dawn,
as the moon sometimes does for the sun.
Be a full bucket pulled up the dark way
of a well, then lifted out into light.

Something opens our wings. Something
makes boredom and hurt disappear.
Someone fills the cup in front of us.
We taste only sacredness.

Rumi
(1207–1273)

Translated by John Moyne and Coleman Barks

FRESH START

Darkness creeps
Over the light of the day;
Hush—
The world is silent now.
A lesser light shines
Over the dark—
God's fantasy of the still night.
The dark engulfs
The sins of the day;
The stars above shout out
To say:
"God forgives and always will;
Tomorrow is another day."

June Cotner, written at age 16

9. Morning

SANSKRIT PROVERB

Look to this day,
For it is life,
The very life of life.
In its brief course lie all
The realities and verities of existence,
The bliss of growth,
The splendor of action,
The glory of power —

For yesterday is but a dream,
And tomorrow is only a vision,
But today, well lived,
Makes every yesterday a dream of happiness
And every tomorrow a vision of hope.

Author unknown

GOD BREATHES

Before dawn
before air ripples the sea
or willows whisper to streams
before leopards stretch
or robins sing —
before creatures
become aware

there is a quickening
a murmur
a movement on the earth
the beat of a distant drum.

God breathes
and one by one we wake.

Mary Lenore Quigley

THE GIFT OF LIFE

Dear God,
Thank you for giving me life, for waking me up, and for giving me the gift of another day. Help me to see the good in other people and to do what is right for the sake of others. Help other people to see what is right, and help them to do no evil. Give me the gift of love, laughter, and everlasting peace. Amen.

Emily Hamer, age 13

EVERY MORNING

Every morning I must realize
That I have the golden opportunity
Of an unused day before me
To use in a divine way.

Sri Chinmoy

PLEASE HELP ME KEEP CALM

Please help me get through the day
and not worry what others say.
I can quickly get very upset.
I hate being so sensitive.
So please help me keep calm
and not worry about everything and everyone.

Kathryn Elizabeth Klein, age 14

ANGEL OF GOD

Angel of God, protect me throughout the day.
Protect me from any harm, fear, or evil that stands in my
    path or disturbs my connection with God. Amen.

David J. Atkins, age 13

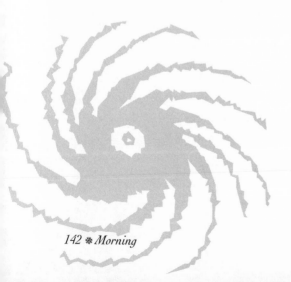

I THANK YOU GOD
FOR MOST THIS AMAZING

i thank You God for most this amazing
day:for the leaping greenly spirits of trees
and a blue true dream of sky;and for everything
which is natural which is infinite which is yes

E. E. Cummings
(1894–1962)

10. Spirituality

REFLECTIONS ON SPIRITUALITY

It is very important to pray for others,
because when you pray for someone,
an angel goes and sits on the shoulder of that person.
Attributed to the Virgin Mary at Medjugore

I get tired of how each religion
looks down on the other.
A visiting pastor once said
knowing God is not a religion,
it is a relationship.
Kristen Eryn Edlund, age 20

We talk about finding God . . . as if He could get lost.
Jerome Horton

People see God every day,
they just don't recognize him.
Pearl Bailey
(1918–1990)

I thank God for my handicaps,
for, through them,
I have found myself, my work, and my God.
Helen Keller
(1880–1968)

A single grateful thought toward heaven
is the most complete prayer.
Gotthold Lessing
(1729–1781)

A PLEDGE,
A PROMISE, AND A PRAYER

I was never taught how to pray. I used to envy my friends who were taught how to talk to God. I hadn't the slightest clue. I would hold long one-sided conversations, but as I have never truly believed in God as an omnipotent, omniscient being, I drew little relief from our "talks." It's only recently I've figured out that I can draw strength and comfort from the beauty in the world around me. Going for a walk in the woods, a sail on the lake, a ride through the fields, or just sitting and being silent so that I can hear the peepers . . . these are my prayers. I see nature as an ultimate power, and whether or not God is behind it all, I am satisfied. Thus with each breath of clean fresh air, I make a pledge, a promise, and a prayer.

Barbara Harrison, age 16

THIS IS HOW
PRAYER SHOULD BE

Flung hands meet the sky.
There is something higher than the stars.
Some place, some final destination.
Feet are rooted to the ground like hundred-year-old
  trees.
Someday they'll run through clouds.
This is how prayer should be, sweet, carefree, and
  spiritual.
I talked to God today.
He told me to be patient, to be kind, to be happy.
This is how prayer should be.

Shelley Johnson, age 17

FOR YOU UNDER A TREE

God—

There's no reason to address you with the solemnity of "DEAR God" because no one uses "Dear" in letters anymore. Everything must be off-handed, as if the speaker could care less, but since you supposedly know everything, you know I am not trying to be too cool or rude. I assume you won't be offended. I also assume that you're ready to listen to me. After all, I've been told in half-whispers and pop hymnals and booming rhetoric that you love me. I just want to know why I don't really fit in. I mean, the children who love you are shining and golden and smiling. I am not, but I think I am still content. This year is the last year of high school for me, and over the summer I asked my religious friends about you. They told me that I must listen closely to you and might find happiness that way, but there was a disconnect between the clarity of their voices and my mind, which groped to understand but failed. They follow you and are the children mothers want and schools are proud of, the ones involved in every aspect of school life. I'm not as involved with the school and don't get along as well with my family as them, so I wonder if I've totally lost contact with you or you're not trying to guide me.

Did I do something as a child to become a lost cause?

Today at school during lunch, I saw my sister sitting on the cement with a group of friends and they were loose and yelling, grinning broadly, eating with sloppy, obvious delight because they were together. I went to the outskirts of the school, slipping behind a row of portable classrooms, and found a place on a mound of dry dirt and grasses. I sat in this spot under the shade of a rotting apple tree (pungent, yellow apples half the size of my fist at my feet) and wondered how I have come to be alone in seventeen years. I talk to people every day, smile, exchange small stories and surprises. But lying in bed at night, before I go to sleep, I do not have anyone to think of. I wonder if I am doing the right thing, what you have planned for me to do, or if there is something wrong with me and I am pushing people away.

There is no urgency to my questions, but I am getting more confused and want to know what you intend for me. I hope you will let me know, though I don't worship you. I do believe you're here, and I'm not sure if I'm deceiving myself by finding peace and goodness in crouching under a tree instead of cheering at Homecoming. Please tell me what there is for me.

Sophia Cheng, age 17

VOICE IN MY SILENCE

I believe that God is in me
as the sun is in the color and fragrance
of a flower —
the Light in my darkness,
the Voice in my silence.

Helen Keller
(1880–1968)

FOR THOSE
WHO ARE LESS FORTUNATE

God,

We sometimes forget that we are more fortunate than others. We have warm homes while others sleep in cardboard boxes. We have full stomachs and throw away leftovers while some go to sleep only dreaming of food. While we are healthily jogging down the street, we pass by those who are ill and dying, lying on our benches. And most important, we have loving families who bring happy memories, while those who are orphaned search for the reason why they were left alone. So, God, give us the strength and compassion to put comfort into the lives of those who are less fortunate.

Steven Asbaghi, age 14

DUSTIN'S TIME

To be behind the wheel
Be free to roam
To reach new places, new people, new thrills.
Rush me on my way, Lord, I cannot wait.

To push my independence forward
Cruise to my future
To speed along through this phase of life
Rush me on my way, Lord, I cannot wait to drive.

My vision of the future has been interrupted
The phone rings—
There has been an accident.

In the night, above a fifty-foot cliff,
unexpectedly, the road curved.

My friend Dustin,
who wanted that same freedom
was found dead in his car.

As his time slowed to a stop,
So did my imagination.
The rushing, the speeding, the cruising . . . is over.

I will proceed with caution, Lord.
For Dustin.

I step from behind the wheel of my fantasy.
I slowly press the accelerator into reality.

Nadia Kourehdar, age 14

FACING ETERNITY

All of us should live life so as to be able
to face eternity at any time.

Heinrich Arnold

I BELIEVE

There is something out there
Amongst the tinfoil stars
Something with intelligence
That made this world of ours

Brendan O'Neill, age 17

ANSWER IN EXTRAORDINARY WAYS

There is a light in this world—a healing spirit—more powerful than any darkness we may encounter. We sometimes lose sight of this force when there is suffering and too much pain. Then suddenly, the spirit will emerge, through the lives of ordinary people who hear a call and answer in extraordinary ways.

Mother Teresa
(1910–1997)

THE PRAYER OF
SAINT FRANCIS OF ASSISI

Lord, make me an instrument of your peace;
Where there is hatred, let me sow love;
Where there is injury, pardon;
Where there is discord, union;
Where there is doubt, faith;
Where there is despair, hope;
Where there is sadness, joy;
Where there is darkness, light.

O Divine Master,
Grant that I may not so much seek to be consoled as
  to console.
Not so much to be understood as to understand.
Not so much to be loved as to love.
For it is in giving that we receive,
In pardoning that we are pardoned,
And in dying that we are born to eternal life.

Saint Francis of Assisi
(1181–1226)

WHATEVER I ENCOUNTER

Lord,
everything in my life
can be a teaching
and a means
of coming closer to you.
Give me the confidence
and the hope
that whatever I encounter
brings me closer
to your will and love.

*Meister Eckhart
(1260–1327)*

THE SERENITY PRAYER

God grant me the serenity
to accept the things I cannot change,
courage to change the things I can,
and wisdom to know the difference.

Reinhold Niebuhr
(1892–1971)

A PUEBLO BLESSING

Hold on to what is good
 Even if it is a handful of earth
Hold on to what you believe
 Even if it is a tree that stands by itself
Hold on to what you must do
 Even if it is a long way from here
Hold on to life
 Even if it is easier to let go
Hold on to my hand
 Even if I have gone away from you

Author unknown

SIOUX PRAYER

Grandfather, Great Spirit, you have been always, and before you nothing has been. There is no one to pray to but you. The star nations all over the heavens are yours, and yours are the grasses of the earth. You are older than all need, older than all pain and prayer. Grandfather, Great Spirit, fill us with the light. Give us the strength to understand and the eyes to see. Teach us to walk the soft earth as relatives to all that live. Help us, for without you we are nothing.

Author unknown

MY SYMPHONY

To live content with small means; to seek elegance
rather than luxury, and refinement rather than fashion;
to be worthy, not respectable, and wealthy, not rich; to
study hard, think quietly, talk gently, act frankly, to
listen to stars and birds, babes and sages, with open
heart; to bear all cheerfully, do all bravely, await
occasions, hurry never. In a word, to let the spiritual,
unbidden and unconscious, grow up through the
common. This is to be my symphony.

William Henry Channing
(1810–1884)

IRISH BLESSING

May the road rise up to meet you.
May the wind be always at your back.
May the sun shine warm upon your face,
The rains fall soft upon your fields.
And until we meet again,
May God hold you in the
Palm of His hand.

Author unknown

GOD IS EVERYTHING

What does God look like?
Everything.
People,
Trees,
Air,
Clouds,
Nothing,
A helping hand,
The world,
The heavens,
Light,
Darkness,
Tranquility,
A nebula,
A supernova,
A budding star,
Water,
Moon,
Sun,
Sky,
Life,
A bird flying.
God is . . .

A night shining,
And the world's first dawn
Brimming with light and warmth.
God will always be here
Like a guiding hand.
God looks like
Love,
God looks like
You,
God looks like
Me,
God looks very caring
To a person as small as me.
God looks almighty and powerful,
To have created us and Earth.
A world without God
Is a world without anything
Because
God is Everything.

Katie Bonacini, age 13

WHAT IF

What if I looked upon every experience with gratitude, thankful for the spiritual growth and lessons that it offered me?

What if I viewed every encounter with every human being as an opportunity to extend my love to them?

What if I viewed everyone as having unlimited potential and wished them only success in their lives?

What if I could see all of the miracles that occur around me in my everyday life?

What if every single day I made a conscious effort to raise my level of awareness, if only by just a little bit?

What if I viewed every person as my student . . . and as my teacher?

What if I accepted everyone for Who They Really Are?

What if I always persisted, when faced with adversity, to bring about a higher truth?

What if Kindness was my way?

What if I never expected anything in return, but was
always joyful for all that I did receive?

What if I never chose out of fear?

What if I loved, in every moment, like God loves?

Deborah Leppanen

I PRAY

I pray for the homeless with nowhere to sleep.
I pray for the hungry with nothing to eat.
I pray for the fearful with no place to hide.
I pray for the hopeless who failed when they tried.
I pray for the sick ones who can't seem to mend.
I pray for the lonely who can't find a friend.
I pray for all the children, those near and those far.
God bless them and keep them wherever they are.

Celia Straus

 # THE ROAD

Here is the road: the light
comes and goes then returns again.
Be gentle with your fellow travelers
as they move through the world of stone and stars
whirling with you yet every one alone.
The road waits.
Do not ask questions but when it invites you
to dance at daybreak, say yes.
Each step is the journey; a single note the song.

Arlene Gay Levine

GO FORTH

Go forth in every direction —
for the happiness, the harmony,
the welfare of the many.
Offer your heart, the seeds of
your own understanding
like a lamp overturned
and re-lit again
illuminating the darkness.

The Buddha
(563–483 B.C.E.)

YOU AND GOD

(This is engraved on the wall of Mother Teresa's home
for children in Calcutta.)

People are often unreasonable, illogical, and self-centered;
forgive them anyway.

If you are kind, people may accuse you of selfish, ulterior
motives; be kind anyway.

If you are successful, you will win some false friends and
some true enemies; succeed anyway.

If you are honest and frank, people may cheat you; be
honest and frank anyway.

What you spend years building, someone could destroy
overnight; build anyway.

If you find serenity and happiness, they may be jealous; be
happy anyway.

The good you do today, people will often forget tomorrow;
do good anyway.

Give the world the best you have, and it may never be enough; give the world the best you've got anyway.

You see, in the final analysis, it is between you and God; it was never between you and them anyway.

Mother Teresa
(1910–1997)

AUTHOR INDEX

Reprinted by permission of Conari Press.

June Cotner for "Fresh Start."

Rachel E. Cox for "God, Thank You for Everything" by Rachel E. Cox from *Looking Past the Sky* by Marilyn Kielbasa. Copyright © 1999 by Saint Mary's Press. Reprinted by permission of Rachel E. Cox.

Creators Syndicate for "Your Talent," an excerpt from a column by Bill O'Reilly. Copyright © 2001 by Bill O'Reilly. Reprinted by permission of Bill O'Reilly and Creators Syndicate.

Denise A. DeWald for "Guard Me from Destructive Thoughts."

Corrine De Winter for "Reflections on Spirituality," "Chrysalis," "Our Wings," "Reflections on Individuality," and "Whole."

Lori Eberhardy for "Angel Embrace" and "The Sacrifice of Halos and Wings."

Kristen Eryn Edlund for "Reflections on Spirituality."

Ida Fasel for "Stopping By a Candy Shelf."

Free Spirit Publishing for "Why Me?" excerpted from the essay "Can Anything Good Come of This" by Bev Cobain in *When Nothing Matters Anymore: A Survival Guide for Depressed Teens* by Bev Cobain, R.N., C. Copyright © 1998. Reprinted by kind permission of Free Spirit Publishing Inc.,

Minneapolis, MN; 1–800–735–7323;
www.freespirit.com. All rights reserved.

HarperCollins Publishers for "The Voice" by Shel
Silverstein from *Falling Up* by Shel Silverstein. This
selection may not be re-illustrated. Copyright ©
1996 by Shel Silverstein. Used by permission of
HarperCollins Publishers.

Barbara Harrison for "A Pledge, a Promise, a Prayer."

Karen Holden for "The Hardest Part Is People."

The Reverend Gary Huffman for "Reflections on
Relationships" and "Deliver Us from Jumping to
Conclusions" by Margaret Anne Huffman. Reprinted
by kind permission of The Reverend Gary Huffman.

Shelley Johnson for "This Is How Prayer Should Be."

Kathryn Elizabeth Klein for "Please Help Me Keep
Calm" by Kathryn Elizabeth Klein from *Looking Past
the Sky* by Marilyn Kielbasa. Copyright © 1999 by
Saint Mary's Press. Reprinted by permission of
Kathryn Elizabeth Klein.

Nadia Kourehdar for "Dialogue of Prayer," "Divorce,"
"Dustin's Time," "I Wonder," and "Mother Nature's
School."

Deborah Leppanen for "What If."

Arlene Gay Levine for "The Road."

Lion Publishing, Oxford, United Kingdom, for "We

Ally Rakoczy for "I'm Never Alone."

Thomas L. Reid for "Courage."

Gail A. Ricciuti for "For All Things," an excerpt from "New Things We Now Declare" by Gail A. Ricciuti in *Birthings and Blessings: Liberating Worship Services for the Inclusive Church* by Rosemary Catalano Mitchell and Gail Anderson Ricciuti. Copyright © 1992 Crossroad. Reprinted by kind permission of Gail A. Ricciuti.

Kate Robinson for "Until the End."

Leah Sell for "Hate to Unite."

Rabbi Rami M. Shapiro for "Unending Love."

The Reverend Dale Turner for "How Much Our Words Mean."

Universal Music Publishing Company for the excerpt from "I Hope You Dance." Words and music by Mark Sanders and Tia Sillers. Copyright © Universal-MCA Music Publishing, a division of Universal Studios, Inc. International copyright secured. All rights reserved.

Whidbey Island Institute for "Reason for Hope," an excerpt from an interview with Jane Goodall by Frances L. Wood, published in the Spring 2001, Vol. 3:1 issue of the *Whidbey Island Institute News*. Copyright © 2001. Reprinted by kind permission of Whidbey Island Institute.

Caitlin R. Woolsey for "A Response to the Holocaust
  Museum."

Father Ralph Wright, O.S.B., for "When God Made
  You" from *Perhaps God* by Father Ralph Wright,
  O.S.B. Copyright © 1985 by Ralph Wright.
  Reprinted by kind permission of Father Ralph
  Wright, O.S.B.

Permissions compiled by Rebecca Pirtle.

FUTURE BOOKS FOR TEENS

I am very excited about hearing from teens for my forthcoming books in the Teen Sunshine series. If you have written poetry that you would like to submit for consideration, I would love to work with you! I am eager to receive work for all three of the following books (listed in order of intended publication):

- TEEN SUNSHINE VOICES: *Poems Written by Teens*
- TEEN SUNSHINE RELATIONSHIPS: *Inspiration and Reflections for All Relationships in a Teen's Life*
- TEEN SUNSHINE REFLECTIONS II: *More Words for the Heart and Soul*

TEEN SUNSHINE VOICES is a collection of poetry that is *written only by teenagers between the ages of thirteen and nineteen*. Teens, this is your chance to get published! (If you are an adult but wrote poems when you were a teen that would work well in these books, feel free to submit them; just be sure to include your age at the time the poem was written.)

TEEN SUNSHINE RELATIONSHIPS will focus on the relationships and interactions that teens have with friends, family, teachers, coaches, and other significant peoples. *All ages are welcome to submit to this book,* but we particularly want to receive submissions from teens.

TEEN SUNSHINE REFLECTIONS II is a continuation of the book you're now holding. *All ages are welcome to submit to this book,* but we particularly welcome submissions from teens.

Please send me a typed copy of the poem with your name, address, phone number, and e-mail address (if you have one) at the top of each page. Include a self-addressed stamped envelope (SASE) to receive a reply. Response time is approximately four months. For teens, *please also indicate your age at the time you wrote the poem.* I hope to hear from you soon!

June Cotner
P.O. Box 2765
Poulsbo, WA 98370
www.junecotner.com
june@junecotner.com